Drama for Students, Volume 33

Project Editor: Sara Constantakis Rights Acquisition and Management: Ashley Maynard, Carissa Poweleit Composition: Evi Abou-El-Seoud Manufacturing: Rhonda Dover

Imaging: John Watkins

Gale
27500 Drake Rd.
Farmington Hills, MI, 48331-3535

ISBN-13: 978-1-4103-1300-3
ISSN 1094-9232

This title is also available as an e-book.
ISBN-13: 978-1-4103-9248-0
ISBN-10: 1-4103-9248-0
Contact your Gale, a part of Cengage Learning sales representative for ordering information.

Printed in Mexico
1 2 3 4 5 6 7 20 19 18 17 16

Disgraced

Ayad Akhtar 2013

Introduction

In Ayad Akhtar's Pulitzer Prize–winning play *Disgraced*, a dinner party involving four successful New Yorkers becomes a tangled nightmare of deceit and anger. The four characters exemplify the harsh reality of the American dream: Amir, a powerful corporate lawyer who keeps his true identity as a Pakistani American a secret from his Jewish bosses; Emily, an idealistic artist whose naiveté is tied to her privilege as an attractive, white woman from a wealthy background; Isaac, a Jewish art curator who manipulates Amir's inner conflict to his own gain with Emily; and Jory, an African American lawyer who raised herself from poverty to become a partner at a law firm through an uncompromising belief in order over emotion. Before the end of the meal, the characters are engaged in a brutal debate that ends in catastrophe. *Disgraced* won the 2013 Pulitzer Prize for Drama and was nominated for the 2015 Tony Award for Best Play.

Author Biography

Ayad Akhtar, A Pakistani American, Was Born On October 28, 1970, On Staten Island, New York, And Was Raised In Milwaukee, Wisconsin. He Studied Theater At Brown University In Rhode Island Before Earning His Master Of Arts Degree In Directing From The Graduate Film Program At Columbia University In New York City. An Actor As Well As A Playwright, Akhtar Studied Acting Under Jerzy Grotowski While Living In Italy After The Completion Of His Undergraduate Degree. Akhtar Cowrote And Starred In The 2005 Film *A War Within*, for which he was nominated for a 2006 Independent Spirit Award for best screenplay. He played Neel Kashkari in HBO's *Too Big to Fail* in 2011.

Disgraced, Akhtar's first major play, premiered at the American Theater Company in Chicago on January 30, 2012. The play went on to open in New York City at the Lincoln Center Theater/LCT3 on October 22, 2012. On May 22, 2013, *Disgraced* made its international premier at London's Bush Theatre. *Disgraced* was awarded the 2013 Pulitzer Prize for Drama and the 2013 Obie Award for playwriting.

Akhtar's second play, *The Invisible Hand* (2012), was awarded the 2015 Outer Critic's Circle Award. His third play, *The Who and the What*, premiered at La Jolla Playhouse in 2014. In addition to his plays, Akhtar has written a novel, *American Dervish*, published in 2012. *Kirkus Reviews, O Magazine, Shelf-Awareness*, and *Globe and Mail* each awarded *American Dervish* the 2012 Best Book of the Year. The novel has been published in more than twenty languages.

Plot Summary

Scene 1

Disgraced is set in a beautiful apartment on New York's affluent Upper East Side. The year is 2011. Inside the apartment is a large marble fireplace, with a statue of Siva, one of the principal gods of Hinduism, displayed on the mantle. Emily, an attractive white woman in her early thirties, sits at the end of the dining room table, sketching a portrait of her husband. Her husband, Amir, is forty years old, of Pakistani heritage. He poses for his wife, wearing an expensive Italian suit jacket, a crisp button-up shirt, and his boxers. He asks if he should put pants on for the portrait.

Emily holds up the painting on which she is basing her portrait—Diego Velâzquez's *Portrait of Juan de Pareja*—to remind him she is drawing him only from the waist up. Amir still finds it strange that she has chosen to represent him in the style of a painting of Velâzquez's slave.

He was Velâzquez's assistant, Emily says; Velâzquez had freed Juan de Pareja from slavery. Emily is drawing in this style because she sees a connection—which Amir does not—between the story behind this painting and an incident that they had experienced at a restaurant the night before. A waiter had been rude to Amir; worse, in Emily's view, he ignored Amir, making assumptions about him because of his race. Amir lets the casual racism of the incident roll off him.

Emily explains that the incident reminded her of Velâzquez's painting. Those who first saw it must have thought they were just looking at a portrait of an assistant (Amir interjects a reminder that Juan de Pareja was a slave), when in fact the portrait is one of Velâzquez's most complex—more so than his portraits of European kings and queens.

She asks Amir to relax and says that no one will see this portrait, but Amir thinks she has gained ground in the New York art scene after her last show and that it is likely to gain some attention. His phone rings—a client calling. He answers. On the phone, he is harsh, forceful, and brutally honest. He tells the client he is not his therapist. Another call comes in, and Amir chastises the paralegal for missing a change in the contract that could have cost his client 850,000 dollars. He hangs up, drifting from his seat to look at the progress of Emily's sketch. Emily likes this ruthless way Amir has of handling business. They kiss.

Amir calls his boss, Mort, to update him on the situation. Emily and Amir fantasize about Amir's making partner at the firm. Emily asks whether Mort thinks Amir is Hindu, because of the statue of Siva he gave him. Amir avoids the question.

Abe, Amir's young nephew, stops by the apartment. Amir calls him by his birth name, Hussein. Abe, exasperated, explains how much easier his life has been since he changed it. When

Amir tries to argue, Abe points out that Amir changed his last name to hide his Muslim heritage as well.

Abe wants Amir's legal help defending his friend, Imam Fareed, who was wrongfully jailed while collecting money for a mosque. Amir tells him that he is not a Muslim, and in any case, he is a corporate lawyer, not a public defender.

Abe tells him his grandmother and mother say that Amir is going through a phase of selfdenial. Amir tells him the story of his first crush: a girl named Rivkah. Amir, who had been raised with values of anti-Semitism (prejudice against Jews), did not realize that Rivkah was a Jewish name. When Amir's mother discovered he was trading notes with a Jewish girl, she spat in Amir's face. The next day at school, when Rivkah confirmed to Amir that she was Jewish, he spat in her face in turn.

After Abe leaves, Emily reminds him that Imam Fareed only wants his own people around him after four months in jail. Amir tells her he does not want to talk about this, and Emily replies that they never do talk about it.

Scene 2

Two weeks later, Emily sits over her morning coffee, reading the newspaper aloud to Amir. Amir is quoted, speaking in support of Imam Fareed's case. He is panicked at the thought that the article implies he is representing Fareed. The paper even mentions the law firm at which he works. Emily does not see the problem. She is proud of the stand Amir took for Fareed's rights. They argue.

As Amir is leaving, Isaac arrives at the apartment to meet with Emily. Isaac is an art curator at the Whitney Museum. He is an attractive Jewish man of Amir's age. The tension between Amir and Emily runs high as he leaves. Isaac jokes that Amir will still get to the firm before his wife, who works as a lawyer there as well.

Left alone with Emily, Isaac admits that he was wrong about his first impression of Emily's work. At first, he had told her she had no right to use Islamic forms as a white woman. He now sees the merit of her work, though he tells her to be prepared for backlash. Some will accuse her of Orientalism— a fetishistic appropriation of Eastern culture— especially considering she is married to Amir. Emily defends her art forcefully, saying it is ludicrous to ignore the influence of the Islamic tradition while embracing the Greeks and Romans. Isaac is impressed.

Scene 3

Three months later, in the fall, Amir stands on the terrace, drinking. Suddenly he smashes the glass on the ground. Still agitated, he goes inside to make himself another drink. Emily arrives, her arms full of groceries. She was getting supplies for that night; Amir had forgotten they are hosting a dinner party, with Isaac and his wife, Jory, as their guests.

Amir apologizes for forgetting, telling her that two of the partners at the law firm walked into his office today and asked where his father was born. They found out that he had misrepresented himself as Indian when in fact his father was born in Pakistan. They also discovered that his last name was Abdullah before he had it changed to Kapoor. Mort is no longer answering his phone calls.

Jory and Isaac arrive much earlier than expected. Emily rushes to the bedroom to get dressed, leaving Amir to greet them. Jory is an African American woman in her late thirties. Jory and Amir talk about work companionably over their drinks, and Amir suggests they break away from the firm and start their own.

Isaac tells Emily that her work will be featured in his newest show at the Whitney: *Impossible Heroes*. Emily is overjoyed. Everyone gives their congratulations. Isaac mentions he is considering using Emily's portrait of Amir. Amir, uncomfortable, says he prefers Emily's landscapes.

Emily says that Amir likes her landscapes best because they have nothing to do with Islam. Isaac defends her work: "A young Western painter drawing on Islamic representation? Not *ironically*? But in *service*? It's an unusual and remarkable statement." They toast to her career.

Jory asks where in India the last name "Kapoor" originates. Amir tells her that the partners asked him the same question today. Emily helps recover from the awkward silence that follows by suggesting the name is Punjabi in origin. Isaac says he is on his way to India in a few days for a studio visit. He mentions he is terrified of flying, and the conversation settles on heightened airport security. Jory asks Amir what it is like for him at the airport. After another awkward pause, Amir admits he volunteers himself to be searched, since he will be racially profiled anyway. Emily finds this behavior extremely passive-aggressive, but Jory admires him for it.

Amir says the next terrorist attack will come from a guy who looks like him. Emily says the next attack will come from a white man with a gun. "And pointing it at a guy that looks like me," Amir adds.

Isaac suggests that the act of giving oneself up to security would seem to justify others' suspicions. Amir asks whether he is suspicious about Middle Easterners. Isaac hesitates, and Amir says he does not blame him. Isaac is bewildered by this stance.

Emily gets a phone call from Abe. Amir admits he had ignored earlier calls from Abe. Emily ignores his call as well. She and Jory go into the kitchen, as dinner is almost ready.

Isaac tries to apologize to Amir, but Amir tells him it is fine. Everyone knows that he and his wife do not agree on the subject of Islam. He does not think art has much to do with the religion. In fact, the Quran states that angels will not enter a house where there are pictures. Emily and Jory return with the salads and join the debate in progress. Amir believes that because it was a religion founded in the desert, Islam is about accepting suffering as a way of life. Isaac points out that the Jewish faith was founded in the desert as well but does not have that attitude. Amir counters that Jewish people used reason and negotiation in order to find a better way to survive in the desert, while Muslims simply submitted. The definition of the world *Islam* is "submission."

Isaac says the problem is not with Islam but with Islamo-facism. The women interrupt, insisting they sit down and eat. Amir says Isaac cannot have an opinion of Islam if he has not read the Quran.

They all dig in to the salad. Isaac compliments the salad, and Emily answers that she found the recipe in Spain. All four at the table have been to Barcelona. Isaac says he does not understand why Amir believes Muslims are so different when he is so similar to Isaac—he would have never known Amir was a Muslim without that article about Fareed's trial.

Amir says he is not a Muslim, he is an apostate —one who has renounced his religion. He says that, according to the Quran, he could be put to death for that offense. Emily says he has not read that part closely enough, proving him wrong. Amir says that wife beating is encouraged. Emily says the translation is unclear. Jory says when given the choice between justice and order, she chooses order. Emily says she would choose justice every time.

After Isaac claims to know many intelligent

Muslim women who choose to wear the veil for modesty, Amir says Isaac does not understand the nuances of Islam because he was not raised in the religion. Isaac says he understands that Amir is full of self-loathing toward his Muslim heritage.

Jory shoots him a glare. Amir ignores the barb, continuing to explain that the Taliban are attempting to re-create the world in the Quran's image. Emily attempts to end the conversation, but Amir does not stop. He explains that to be Muslim is to feel pride in the purity of emotion in those willing to act out those beliefs.

Isaac asks whether Amir felt pride on learning of the terrorist attacks of September 11, 2001. Amir, after hesitating, says yes. The table is in an uproar. Emily says he does not mean that. Jory asks what about the attacks, exactly, made Amir proud.

"That we were finally winning," Amir says and admits he forgot which "we" he belonged to at the time. He says it was a tribal feeling, a result of his upbringing. Emily has had enough; she disappears into the kitchen.

After a long, uncomfortable silence at the dining room table, Amir attempts to make amends by comparing his emotions to those Isaac must feel toward Israel as a Jewish man. Isaac says he does not support Israel. Amir asks how he feels when he hears threats against Israel. Isaac says he is outraged by the violence in the Middle East, like most people. Amir says that some people like hearing those threats; upon prompting by Isaac, Amir admits that he sometimes is one of those people.

Desperate to change the subject, Emily reminds Amir that they are supposed to be celebrating. Amir ignores her. He says that the feeling he gets, the blush of pride, is wrong, and it comes from being raised Muslim.

Isaac says the pride comes from Amir alone, that Islam does not own fundamentalism any more than any other religion in the world and that the generalizations Amir makes so easily are frightening.

Jory tells Isaac to stop arguing, and he does. Amir calls him naïve. Emily tells him to come with her into the kitchen. Left alone at the table, Jory asks why Isaac keeps picking fights with Amir. Isaac calls Amir a closet jihadist. Jory says Amir is not acting like himself, and wonders if he knows her secret. She decides she needs to tell him, that he deserves to hear it from her.

Amir bursts from the kitchen door, grabbing his coat in preparation to leave. He says he is going out to get champagne, so that they can celebrate Emily's involvement in the art show. Jory grabs her coat to go with him to the store.

As soon as they leave, Emily turns on Isaac, and they argue: it becomes clear that they had been romantically involved. Isaac suspects her of sleeping with him only to get into the art show, and she retorts that if that is the reason she got in, she does not want to be included. Twice he tries to touch her; she pulls away quickly the first time, but more slowly the next time.

Isaac asks whether Amir knows about Jory's promotion to partner. Emily is shocked. Isaac says Amir was passed over because of his association with Fareed, which Isaac considers a foolish decision. Emily says he did it for her sake.

Isaac tells her he is in love with her and leans in to kiss her. Emily holds still. Jory enters. She takes in the scene in front of her and demands an explanation. Amir enters behind her in a rage, hurt that Jory took so long to tell him about her promotion. Jory, ignoring him, asks Emily bluntly if she is having an affair with Isaac. Isaac and Emily both deny it, but Jory tells Amir she saw them kissing.

Amir accuses Jory of trying to destroy his marriage as well as his career, and he spits in Isaac's face and tells Jory to get out. She leaves, but not before telling Amir that Mort does not trust him.

Alone, Amir asks Emily if she is sleeping with Isaac. She admits it happened once, but she is disgusted by her behavior. He hits her in the face, multiple times, viciously, just as someone starts to knock at the front door. When the knocking goes unanswered, the door opens slowly to reveal Abe, who takes in the scene in front of him in shock.

Scene 4

Six months later, in the spring of 2012, the apartment is nearly empty except for moving boxes.

Emily's paintings are absent, except for a small, covered canvas leaning against the wall. Amir, alone, is packing. He answers a knock at the door to find Emily and Abe, who is now dressed in muted, conservative colors and a Muslim skullcap. Abe cannot meet Amir's eyes. Emily explains to Amir that Abe was stopped by the FBI after a friend he was with made a scene, telling a waitress who asked if they were Muslims that the Americans created al-Qaeda. His friend Tariq lost his patience with her questions and told her that America deserved what happened. The police arrived and took Abe and Tariq to the station, where two men from the FBI were waiting.

Emily attempts to leave, but Abe begs her to stay. Reluctantly, she agrees, though she goes to the kitchen rather than remain in the room. Amir tells Abe that he needs to remember that the world is not neutral toward him. Abe suggests that Amir should spend more time with his own people, but Amir says he will get deported if he remains so careless. Abe reveals that he knows Amir was fired, and he knows what Amir did to Emily. He says Amir has forgotten who he is. Amir, disbelieving, reminds Abe that he has changed his name to Abe Jensen to blend in to American society. Abe says he changed his name back, but Amir is unimpressed.

Abe says Amir will always turn on his own people and that those outside his community do not respect him more for it. They think that he hates himself, and Abe thinks they are right. Abe gains steam, saying that it is pointless to try to live by society's rules. He believes Muslims who attempt to assimilate with non-Muslim cultures have disgraced Islam and that it is the destiny of Muslims to take the world back. Emily enters the room, and Abe, realizing that she has been listening, leaves abruptly.

Amir asks Emily whether she has read his letters. He got the painting from her. Emily says she did not want to throw it out. Amir says he wants Emily to get their apartment in the divorce, but Emily does not want it. Amir says he finally understands her art, but Emily says her art was naïve. Emily says she played a role in what happened between them, that she was selfish. Amir says no; he wants Emily to be proud of him and to be proud that she was with him. Emily asks him to stop writing to her. She leaves. Amir uncovers the painting—Emily's portrait of him—and stares searchingly at the canvas.

Jory Brathwaite

Jory, an African American woman in her late thirties, is the newest partner at Leibowitz, Bernstein, and Harris. She is Isaac's wife. She and Amir get along well at the office, though she does not tell Amir about her promotion right away because she knows he had also wanted the job. Jory attributes her success to her ability to value order over justice. She is straightforward with her opinions and emotions. When she discovers her husband kissing Emily, she confronts them both immediately. She leaves the dinner party after telling Amir that no one trusts him at the office. Their friendship is ruined by the revelation that she has gotten the promotion instead of him.

Imam Fareed

Fareed is a friend of Abe's who is wrongfully in jail awaiting trial for collecting money for a terrorist organization. In fact, Fareed was collecting money for a mosque. Abe begs Amir to appear in court in support of Fareed. It is Amir's first instinct to avoid association with a suspected terrorist, but Emily encourages him to support Fareed. He appears at his trial and is quoted by the newspaper making a passionate argument in Fareed's defense. This leads to his falling out at the law firm where he works.

Emily Hughes-Kapoor

Emily is a painter who incorporates Islamic tile patterns and architectural elements into her work. She is married to Amir, with whom she disagrees on the nature of the Muslim religion. Emily and Isaac have an affair in London while attending an art fair. She is very excited and happy to learn that she will be included in Isaac's upcoming show at a prominent art gallery, though she is upset by Isaac's argumentative behavior toward her husband during their dinner party. After Jory catches Isaac and Emily embracing, Emily admits her infidelity to Amir. He beats her and is caught in the act by Abe. Emily does not press charges against Amir, though they do divorce. Emily does not want the apartment and gives the portrait she painted of Amir to him rather than throw it out.

Isaac

Isaac is a forty-year-old art curator at the Whitney Museum. He is an attractive Jewish man who is perplexed by Emily's art. He feels at first that she has no place as a white woman in using Islamic forms, but she convinces him that Islamic art is like Greek or Roman art in that it is ancient and part of humanity's shared history. Isaac is married to Jory. He cheats on his wife with Emily and then adds Emily to his art show at the Whitney. At the dinner party, Isaac provokes Amir by drawing him into arguments throughout the night. When he is left alone with Emily he tells her he loves her and tries to kiss her. Jory catches them, revealing the affair.

Abe Jensen

Abe Jensen is Amir's twenty-two-year-old nephew, the son of his sister. Abe is a practicing Muslim, like the rest of Amir's family. He turns to Amir for help after his friend, Imam Fareed, is wrongfully imprisoned. When Abe first appears, he is dressed in the modern fashion of a young American and has recently changed his name from Hussein to Abe to escape discrimination. He is idealistic and indefatigable, calling Emily when Amir ignores his calls. He witnesses the aftermath of the disastrous dinner party, walking in the apartment to find Emily bleeding after Amir has beaten her. The next time Abe appears, he has changed his name back to Hussein and dresses in a Muslim skullcap and muted colors. The FBI interrogates him after he and a friend cause a scene at a Starbucks. He is at risk for deportation.

However, Abe no longer wants Amir's help and has trouble looking him in the eye.

José

Joséis Emily's ex-boyfriend, a black Spanish man who speaks little English.

Amir Kapoor

Amir is a successful corporate lawyer at Leibowitz, Bernstein, and Harris. He is married to Emily. He changed his last name from Abdullah to Kapoor in order to avoid discrimination against Arab Americans. At the office, he pretends to be an Indian American. He was brought up in a strict Muslim household but has renounced his religion. Amir is deeply troubled by his Muslim heritage and is quick to make negative generalizations about the religion and its practitioners. Both Isaac and Abe accuse him of hating himself. Once Amir is quoted in defense of Imam Fareed, the partners at the law firm begin to realize he has lied about his background. He is eventually fired after bursting out in tears during a meeting. Amir struggles with his own aggressive nature but attributes it to his Muslim upbringing. At the dinner party, already on edge because of the discovery of his heritage at work, Amir argues with Isaac over what it means to be Muslim and the nature of Islam, as well as his own rejection of the religion. Amir beats Emily after she admits to her affair, acting out one of the passages he finds most offensive in the Quran. After the dinner party, Amir has lost Jory as a friend, Abe's respect, and Emily. He is left staring at Emily's portrait of him, lost as to his own identity.

Hussein Malik

See Abe Jensen

Mort

Mort is Amir's boss, who gave Amir a Siva statue as a present, thinking he was Hindu. Mort and Amir are close until the newspaper article about Fareed is published. Mort stops taking Amir's calls afterward. Jory reveals that Mort is retiring and Jory will be taking on his caseload, not Amir.

Rivkah

Rivkah is Amir's first love. She is a pretty classmate from sixth grade with whom he shared his first kiss. Amir's mother discovers a love note Rivkah has written to Amir and tells her son she will not allow him to become involved with a Jewish girl. Amir does not fully understand why his mother disapproves of Jewish people, so he simply tries to deny that she is Jewish. His mother spits in his face. The next day at school, when Rivkah approaches to give Amir another note, Amir tells her she has a Jewish name. When Rivkah states that she is Jewish, Amir spits in her face.

Steven

Steven is a partner at the law firm where Jory and Amir work. Jory tells Amir that Steven, not Mort, holds the real power at the firm. Steven asks Amir about his heritage on the day of the dinner party, revealing that the firm has discovered Amir's deception.

Tariq

Tariq is Abe's friend. After an argument with a waitress, he shouts inside a Starbucks that the United States deserved what it got in the terrorist attacks, and it deserved what it would get in the future. As a result, he and Abe are arrested and taken to the police station, where two FBI agents are waiting to interrogate them.

Themes

Anger

Ten years after the 9/11 terrorist attacks, Amir is still aware of the target on his back as a Pakistani American and former Muslim. In the play's opening scene, Amir and Emily have just had an encounter with a racist waiter, Emily is painting a portrait of Amir based on a slave, and Amir's family—Emily and Abe—are begging him to represent in court a man accused of fund raising for an Islamic extremist organization. Amir feels safer falsifying his identity than admitting his background at work, despite his professionalism, his years of hard work, and his good standing with the firm. Amir, an American success story, is associated every day with 9/11, terrorism, and radical Islam. The constant pressure of living in an Islamophobic society has turned Amir sour, passive-aggressive, and angry. His anger is internalized, taking the form of self-hatred, for most of the play. Viewed with suspicion by the world around him ("duplicitous," as Jory describes him), he knows that acting out his anger will only prove those who judge him right. Instead, he gives in to the outside pressures—posing as a peaceful Hindu, giving himself up to airport security—while allowing the anger he represses to eat away at him from the inside out. As a powerful American man, he believes he should be enjoying a well-earned life of luxury without dragging the weight of his cultural identity behind him. But in a climate of suspicion and fear, he is not free. He cannot take on a charity case for his nephew without being thought to be a terrorist sympathizer, just as Fareed cannot collect money for a mosque without being jailed for four months on vague charges, just as Tariq cannot throw a fit in a Starbucks without being interrogated afterward by the FBI. The Muslim characters of *Disgraced* are chained to their religious identity in the eyes of society, but any anger that they express is harshly punished.

Topics for Further Study

- Research Islamic art and architecture online. Create a blog featuring five works of Islamic art or architecture that you admire. Include photos, background information about the work, and where it can be found. Also choose an artistic or architectural term relevant to each of the works to define (for example, *arabesque, symmetry,* or *minaret*). Free blog space is available at http://www.blogspot.com.

- Read Marina Budhos's young-adult novel *Ask Me No Questions* (2007) about a teenaged Muslim girl living in New York City as an undocumented alien. Compare and contrast Nadra's life and Amir's. How does some Americans' fear or hatred of Muslim people following the terrorist attacks of September 11, 2001, affect their lives? What struggles are unique to their individual situations? Organize your thoughts into a comparative essay.

- In a small group, perform a two-to five-minute selection from *Disgraced*, with one member of the group acting as director. Film and edit the video as a group, using the tools found on http://www.edpuzzle.com.

- Write an additional scene for *Disgraced* that takes place in the months between scene 3 and scene 4, illustrating one of the results of the dinner party. For example, you could chose to write a scene showing Emily's decision to move out, Amir's last day at the law office, Abe's changing personal style, or a scene involving Isaac and Jory's relationship. Use your imagination and remember to include stage directions as well as dialogue.

- Choose a character other than Amir who plays a role in the climactic dinner party to examine more closely. What is that person's attitude at the beginning of the scene? What topics of conversation are of the most interest? How does this person react to the growing tension, and does he or she encourage the tension or discourage it? What has changed for this person by the end of the scene? Summarize your observations in a brief essay.

Identity

Amir's struggle with identity drives the play from its first moments to the final curtain. Born in Pakistan and raised in a proud Muslim family, Amir lives an affluent American lifestyle as a vocal critic of Islam. Yet he remembers the lessons his mother taught him, such as the story of his first crush on a Jewish girl named Rivkah. As a child, he spit in the girl's face, parroting his mother's hatred. As an adult, he pretends to be an Indian at work to avoid upsetting the Jewish partners with the truth of his heritage. There is no balance to Amir's identity. His childhood instruction tugs him in one direction, and his fierce adult determination tugs him in another direction, creating a tangle of confused emotions: anger, shame, pride, and pain. This war within Amir is no secret. His family, his wife, even his coworkers and acquaintances share their opinions of who he is and how he should act. To Emily, Amir is a Muslim "in a way that's unique." Amir rejects this assessment at once. Amir's mother claims that his rejection of Islam is a phase, a theory of Amir's behavior that she passed on to Amir's sister, who in turn teaches it to Abe. To Isaac, Amir is a "closet jihadist," implying he is potentially violent, an extremist.

Abe tells Amir, in the final scene: "You'll always turn on your own people. You think it makes these people like you more when you do that? They don't. They just think you hate yourself. And they're right!" Though Amir begins the play a confident, powerful lawyer with the apartment to match, trouble takes the form of the portrait Emily makes of him, based on Velâzquez's freed slave, Juan de Pareja. Amir finds the connection that Emily sees between himself and the slave disturbing, just as he later changes the subject when she attempts to discuss his Muslim background. Amir wants to be seen as a successful American man, not a Muslim, not an underdog, and not a victim. He has achieved the American dream, an immigrant who has risen to the top of his field, but the political environment after 9/11 conspires to keep his Middle Eastern and

Islamic heritage front and center, a red hot issue preventing anyone—but especially Amir himself—from forgetting the past that he so disdains. While the other characters have complex views of Islam, none are as full of contradictions, memories, and bewildered emotions as Amir's, so much so that Islam is tied directly to Amir's identity. The repression of that identity leads directly to his collapse.

Climax

The climax of a work of literature is the point of highest tension or a decisive moment, and it occurs at the peak of the rising action, usually near the end of a story. For example, the climax of *Disgraced* is the argument at the conclusion of the dinner party that ends in Amir's beating Emily. The climax is the result of the building tensions throughout the night: Amir's fear of losing his job over falsifying his background, Jory's secret promotion, and Isaac and Emily's affair. The climax brings all secrets into the open and reveals what the characters truly think of one another. Akhtar engineers the especially shocking climax of *Disgraced* through the progressively antagonistic dinner conversation between Amir and Isaac, building tension as both Emily and Jory try and fail to end the discussion. The party separates in an attempt to cool hot heads, but Jory's discovery of the affair between Emily and Isaac brings the climax crashing down to disastrous conclusion.

Denouement

Denouement is a French term literally meaning "untying." In a work of literature, the denouement is the resolution or conclusion of a story in which the results of the climax are described, plots are resolved, and characters are shown to have changed for the better or worse. Scene 4 makes up the denouement of *Disgraced*. Taking place six months after the dinner party, the scene shows the results of the actions of the four characters that night. The denouement mainly concerns the dissolution of Amir and Emily's relationship, leaving Amir staring at the portrait that began the play as if questioning his identity. In this way, the denouement finalizes the plot, while placing an emphasis on the ways in which the characters have changed as a result of the climax.

September Eleventh

In the heat of their argument at the dinner party, Isaac asks Amir if he felt pride on September 11. *Disgraced* deals both directly and indirectly with the experience of Middle Eastern Americans in the post-9/11 environment. On the morning of September 11, 2001, nineteen members of the Islamic extremist group al-Qaeda carried out terrorist attacks on the World Trade Center in downtown Manhattan and the Pentagon in Arlington, Virginia, killing more than three thousand people. The attacks, referred to simply as 9/11 or September 11, involved four airliners, three of which the terrorists hijacked and crashed into their targets: the north and south Twin Towers, which collapsed from the resulting damage, and the Pentagon. Though the fourth airliner was similarly hijacked and turned off course toward an unknown target on the Eastern Seaboard, the passengers successfully revolted, crashing the plane into a field in Pennsylvania.

Fifteen of the terrorists were from Saudi Arabia, two from the United Arab Emirates, and one each from Lebanon and Egypt. They carried knives and box cutters through airport security and then used these weapons to take over the planes. The attack was symbolic, as the World Trade

Center, with its massive twin skyscrapers, represented the height of American global power. As a result of the attack, the "war on terror" was launched, seeking to wipe out terrorist cells in the Middle East, as well as a manhunt for al-Qaeda's leader, Osama bin Laden. A defining moment in the history of the United States, September 11 changed the country both drastically and instantaneously. Martin Kettle writes in the British newspaper *Guardian*, "I covered American politics for the *Guardian* for four years from 1997. I moved back to Britain towards the end of August 2001. Three weeks later, the country I had lived in ceased to exist."

Islam and Islamophobia Post-9/11

No group felt the changes following the September 11 terrorist attacks more keenly than Middle Eastern Americans. Muslims and people who were perceived as being Muslim fell victim to suspicion, prejudice, and violence simply as a result of their superficial resemblance to the members of al-Qaeda. In reality, Islam is the second-largest religion in the world, with more than a billion followers. Based on the teachings of the prophet Muhammad, passed down in the Quran (alternately spelled Qur'an or Koran), the religion is monotheistic, with the worship of God as its centerpiece. Like Christianity and Hinduism, Islam is divided into denominations, and those denominations are further divided. Islamic extremists make up a small percentage of the much larger Muslim population.

Islamophobia, an irrational fear and hatred of Muslims, spread across the United States overnight following the attacks. In 2001, hate crimes against Muslims increased 1,700 percent from the previous year. Fueled by their ignorance concerning the differences between the religion of Islam and Islamic extremism, Islamophobic individuals tend to view all Muslims as dangerous and anti-American. Islamophobia appears throughout *Disgraced*, from the wrongful imprisonment of Imam Fareed, whose collections for a new mosque are mistaken for collections for a terrorist organization, to Amir's experience with heightened airport security.

Critical Overview

Disgraced won the 2013 Pulitzer Prize for Drama, and the Broadway production was nominated in 2015 for the Tony Award for Best Play. *Disgraced* has been widely praised by critics since its debut in 2012. Stefanie Cohen, in her interview of Akhtar for the *Wall Street Journal*, calls him "the de facto voice of the American Muslim in theater."

Critics have been particularly enamored of the contrast between the sophisticated dinner party setting and the brutal behavior of those seated at the table. The *New Yorker* calls *Disgraced* a "smart, sharp-edged play ... cocktail hour gone bananas." In his interview of Akhtar for *PBS NewsHour*, Jeffrey Brown praises the play's emotional range, which keeps the audience uncomfortable but engaged: "There's plenty of humor in *Disgraced*, but quite a bit more pain, as Amir's world and identity comes undone." Stephen Moss characterizes Amir's battle in his interview with Akhtar for the *Guardian*: "American v. Asian, Muslim v. secularist, passive observer of injustice v. activist."

Charles Isherwood, in a review for the *New York Times*, "Beware Dinner Talk on Identity and Islam," admires the social depth of the play's themes. He calls it "a continuously engaging, vitally engaged play about thorny questions of identity and religion in the contemporary world ... [and] the incendiary topic of how radical Islam and the terrorism it inspires have affected the public discourse."

The play has seen successful runs in Chicago, New York, and London. In a time when issues of terrorism and Islamic extremism are consistently in the news, *Disgraced* vividly illustrates the effects of fear, anger, and discrimination. Writing for *Variety*, Marilyn Stasio describes *Disgraced* as "an intellectually engaging play on a politically provocative topic."

What Do I Read Next?

- Banned in Saudi Arabia, Abdelrahman Munif's *Cities of Salt* (1987) describes the disastrous results following America's discovery of oil in a small village in an unnamed country in the Middle East.

- In *American Dervish* (2012), Akhtar's first novel, the life of Hayat Shah, a typical American teenager, is changed forever when he falls for Mina, his mother's friend from Pakistan. Mina teaches Hayat about Islam, opening up a brilliant new world for him where before there had been only video games and school. But when Mina begins to date a new man, Hayat acts out on his heartbreak, with a disastrous result.

- In Mohsin Hamid's novel *The Reluctant Fundamentalist* (2007), Changez is living a charmed life in America, a Princeton graduate with a high-status job at a firm in Manhattan. But as he watches the Twin Towers collapsing on September 11, he is surprised to find himself smiling. His life overturned, Changez returns home to Pakistan to discover who he is and what he has become.

- *American Islam: The Struggle for the Soul of a Religion*, by Paul M. Barrett (2007), dispels the myths and assumptions surrounding the six million Muslims living in the United States by giving an intimate, journalistic account of seven

American Muslim lives.

- *Brick Lane*, by Monica Ali (2003), tells the story of Nazneen, a Bangladeshi child bride brought by her new husband to live in London. Nazneen finds her own voice so many miles from the familiarity of home amidst the chaos following the September 11 terrorist attacks and their wide-reaching effects in England.

- In Michael Muhammad Knight's *The Taqwacores* (2004) a group of young Muslims in Buffalo, New York, merge Islam and punk rock in their run-down apartment. Taking their name from the Arabic word for a "consciousness of the divine," *taqwa*, the Taqwacores fuse riotous parties with earnest worship.

- Rajaa Alsanea's novel *Girls of Riyadh* (2005) features four wealthy Saudi Arabian women who must navigate the treacherous gap between their modern lives and the harsh restrictions on women in their society.

- *Does My Head Look Big in This?*, by Randa Abdel-Fattah (2005), is a young-adult novel about sixteen-year-old Amal's decision to wear the hijab and the way her life changes as a result of her devotion to her religion.

- *Qur'an and Woman: Rereading the Sacred Text from a Woman's Perspective*, by Amina Wadud (1999), provides the first published interpretation of the Qur'an written by a woman, with a specific focus on those passages that have been used to dictate what is proper feminine behavior under Islamic laws.

- *The Good Muslim*, by Tahmima Anam (2011), features an irreconcilable feud between a brother and sister over religious fundamentalism, set in the decade following a civil war in Bangladesh.

———————————————

Sources

Akhtar, Ayad, *Disgraced*, Back Bay Books, 2013.

Brown, Jeffrey, "*Disgraced* Interrogates Definitions of Identity and Islam in America," PBS website, October 30, 2014, http://www.pbs.org/newshour/bb/disgraced-interrogates-definitions-identity-islam-america/ (accessed June 29, 2015).

Cohen, Stefanie, "*Disgraced* Playwright: 'I'm Writing about the American Experience,'" in *Wall Street Journal*, November 7, 2014, http://www.wsj.com/articles/disgraced-playwright-ayad-akhtar-im-writing-about-the-american-experience-1415365558 (accessed June 29, 2015).

"FAQ about 9/11," National September 11 Memorial and Museum website, http://www.911memorial.org/faq-about-911 (accessed July 10, 2015).

Isherwood, Charles, "Beware Dinner Talk on Identity and Islam," in *New York Times*, October 22, 2012, http://www.nytimes.com/2012/10/23/theater/reviews by-ayad-akhtar-with-aasif-mandvi.html (accessed June 9, 2015).

"Islamophobia: Understanding Anti-Muslim Sentiment in the West," Gallup.com, 2015, http://www.gallup.com/poll/157082/islamophobia-understanding-anti-muslim-sentiment-west.aspx (accessed July 10, 2015).

Kamp, David, "Rethinking the American Dream," in *Vanity Fair*, April 2009, http://www.vanityfair.com/culture/2009/04/american dream200904 (accessed October 21, 2015).

Kettle, Martin, "What Impact Did 9/11 Have on America?," in *Guardian*, September 6, 2011, http://www.theguardian.com/commentisfree/cifamer 9-11-america (accessed July 10, 2015).

Khan, Muqtedar, "American Muslims Should Fight Islamophobia in 2016 Elections," *Al Jazeera America* website, April 18, 2015, http://america.aljazeera.com/opinions/2015/4/americ muslims-should-fight-islamophobiain-2016-elections.html (accessed July 10, 2015).

Moss, Stephen, "Pulitzer Playwright Ayad Akhtar: 'I Was in Denial,'" in *Guardian*, May 7, 2013, http://www.theguardian.com/stage/2013/may/07/pul playwright-ayad-akhtar (accessed June 29, 2015).

"9/11 Attacks: Facts & Summary," in *History.com*, 2010, http://www.history.com/topics/9-11-attacks (accessed July 10, 2015).

Review of *Disgraced* in *New Yorker*, http://www.newyorker.com/goings-on-about-town/theatre/disgraced-2 (accessed June 29, 2015).

Rose, Steve, "Since 9/11, Racism and Islamophobia Remain Intertwined," in *Huffington Post*, December 9, 2013, http://www.huffingtonpost.co.uk/steve-rose/911-racism-islamophobia_b_3908411.html (accessed July 12, 2015).

Stasio, Marilyn, "Broadway Review: *Disgraced*," in *Variety*, October 23, 2014, http://variety.com/2014/legit/reviews/broadway-review-disgraced-josh-radnor-1201337499 (accessed June 9, 2015).

Further Reading

Akhtar, Ayad, *The Who And The What*, Back Bay Books, 2014.

> In Akhtar's 2014 play, Zarina, daughter of a strict Muslim family living in Atlanta, Georgia, writes a daring novel about wearing the veil that threatens to tear her conservative family apart.-

Cottee, Simon, *The Apostates: When Muslims Leave Islam*, Hurst, 2015.

> Cottee looks into the lives of Muslims in the West who have given up their faith, a controversial topic in Islam and one whose consequences in the West are rarely explored.

Gray, Richard, *After the Fall: American Literature since 9/11*, Wiley-Blackwell, 2011.

> Gray's work focuses on the changes in American culture and literature following the September 11, 2001, terrorist attacks, with a particular interest in those literary voices that have resisted the temptation to simplify the world after 9/11 as a war between "us" and "them."

Green, Todd H., *The Fear of Islam: An Introduction to Islamophobia in the West*, Fortress Press, 2015.

Green traces the origins of Islamophobia throughout history to learn more about Western society's struggles with prejudice against Muslims today, emphasizing the role of the conflict between Israel and Palestine in stifling discussions that should be open and honest.